I AM A MOST SUPERIOR PERSON

The World's Greatest Egomaniacs
Outrageously Explained by Themselves
and Others

Gathered by William Cole

ST. MARTIN'S PRESS
NEW YORK

Production Editor: David Stanford Burr

The caricatures in this edition are from various collections by
Grandville, né Jean Ignace Isidore Gerárd (1803–1847).

Library of Congress Cataloging-in-Publication Data

I am a most superior person : the world's greatest egomaniacs
   outrageously explained by themselves and others / William
   Cole, editor.
         p.   cm.
   "A Thomas Dunne book."
   ISBN 0-312-13515-7
   1. Quotations.   2. Quotations, English.   3. Wit and
humor.   I. Cole, William.
PN6081.I14   1995
082—dc20   95-34570
                                                        CIP

First edition: October 1995

10   9   8   7   6   5   4   3   2   1

CONTENTS

★

INTRODUCTION

★

My name is George Nathaniel Curzon,
I am a most superior person;
My cheek is pink, my hair is sleek,
I dine at Blenheim once a week.

This famous anonymous rhyme was about Lord Curzon of Kedleston (1859–1925), a British statesman, author, and Viceroy of India. His chilling reserve, monocle, and studied hauteur made him almost a caricature of the English aristocrat. And Blenheim Palace, near Oxford, was the family seat of the Duke of Marlborough, a gathering place for the elite. Curzon is in many quotation books for his remark, upon seeing soldiers bathing, "I never knew the lower classes had such white skins."

Curzon wasn't entirely humorless, however. Witness his clever reply to the poem about him above:

Charms and a man I sing, to wit—a most
    superior person,
Myself who bears the fitting name of George
    Nathaniel Curzon,
From which 'tis clear that even when in
    swaddling bands I lay low,
There floated round my head a sort of
    apolistic halo.

Each person, we know, considers himself the center of the universe. Thus it is not surprising that some hold that opinion to excess. The people we hear from in this gallimaufry may be divided into geniuses, blow-hards, and leg-pullers. I take particular pleasure in the leg-pullers—the jokers—such as Mark Twain, Sir Noel Coward, and Raymond Chandler. Chief among the self-proclaimed geniuses—who meant it—are one literary gent and two ladies, clustered together under the letter *S*—one genius, Shaw, and two fakers, Stein and Sitwell.

In researching, I was surprised to find so many poets heralding themselves. Robert Frost, for example, who always presented himself as a lovable grandfatherly country philosopher, was in reality fiercely envious of other poets and had an ego you couldn't crack with a sledge-hammer. I know a contemporary poet who is actually known for "preening" in public. Unfortunately he hasn't put it in writing. I also couldn't find a quotation in print by that supreme egotist—and bad writer—of the western world, the dreaded J. P. Donlevy, who is reputed to have, in his Irish country house, only books written by himself. The critic Patrick Skene Catling, reviewing J. P.'s recent history of *The Ginger Man*, coined a new and necessary word, writing, ". . . an extravagantly enthusiastic auto-hagiography that makes John Osborne seem moderate and Norman Mailer modest." These self-exalters are cause for guffaws; they actually seem to believe what they say!

The prize blow-hard of all time was the biographer, autobiographer, and magazine editor, Frank Harris, an odd, dwarfish man, famous for saying "Christ went deeper than I, but I have had a wider range of experience." Surely that can't be matched by either Dali or Ali.

I've always wondered, in a diffident sort of way, about the difference between "egotism" and "egoism." In my basic desk dictionary, "egotism" is "excessive use of the first person singular pronoun," (or the great *I-am*.) "Egoism" is "a doctrine that individual self-interest is the actual motive of all conscious action." They're both here in abundance.

If I had to choose one favorite quotation from among these hundreds, I would pick the last words of the French philosopher, Auguste Comte (1798–1857). I think he spoke for all of us when, at the dying of the light, he murmured, "What an irreparable loss."

—WILLIAM COLE

I love me, I love me, I'm wild about myself,
I love me, I love me, my picture's on the shelf,
You may not think I look so good but me thinks I'm just
   fine
It's grand when I look in my eye and knows that I'm all
   mine.

Oh I love me and my love doesn't bore
Day by day in every way I love me more and more
I takes me to a quiet place I puts my arms around my
   waist
If me gets fresh I slap my face, I'm wild about myself.

> — FROM AN ENGLISH SONGBOOK,
> QUOTED IN E. M. FORSTER'S
> *COMMONPLACE BOOK*

All the passions are extinguished with old age; self-love
never dies.

> —AMERICAN PROVERB

To say that a man is vain merely means that he is pleased
with the effect he produces on other people. A conceited
man is satisfied with the effect he produces on himself.

> —MAX BEERBOHM

The advantage of doing one's praising for oneself is that
one can lay it on so thick and exactly in the right places.

> —SAMUEL BUTLER

Only the good-for-nothings are modest.

—GEORGE LANG

When you would hurt a man keenest, strike at his self-love.

—LEW WALLACE

I am, in point of fact, a particularly haughty and exclusive person, of pre-Adamite ancestral descent . . . my family pride is something inconceivable. I can't help it. I was born sneering.

—POOH-BAH IN *THE MIKADO*
SIR W. S. GILBERT

I AM A MOST SUPERIOR PERSON

★

I
ACTORS

". . . incredibly sexy, intelligent and articulate."

★

JOHN BARRYMORE

I like to be introduced as America's foremost actor. It saves the necessity of further effort.

★

One of my chief regrets during my years in the theater is that I couldn't sit in the audience and watch me.

SARAH BERNHARDT

Sarah took it for granted that she was the greatest actress in the world, just as Queen Victoria took it for granted that she was Queen of England.

—Maurice Baring

TRUMAN CAPOTE

What Dom Perignon is to champagne, I am to acting.

DAVID CARRADINE

I'm perhaps the most gifted actor of my generation.

JOHN CASSAVETES

It's bullshit when people say that ego is a bad trip. It's the *only* trip. You are who you are because of your ego; without it nothing counts.

DICK CAVETT

We haven't ruled out the possibility of children but I figure I'm the blessed event in our family.

CHARLIE CHAPLIN

I am known in parts of the world by people who have never heard of Jesus Christ.

SIR NOEL COWARD

I am an enormously talented man, after all it's no use pretending that I am not, and I was bound to succeed.

BETTE DAVIS

There's only one of us in each country.

PATRICK DEMPSEY
actor playing JFK on TV special

I'm incredibly sexy, intelligent and articulate. There are so many similarities, it's amazing.

TO INTERVIEWER (JOKING)

VITTORIO GASSMAN

He used to grab me in his arms, hold me close—and tell me how wonderful he was.

—SHELLEY WINTERS

JACKIE GLEASON

I have no use for humility. I am a fellow with an exceptional talent.

JERRY HALL
model, Mick Jagger companion

I think if I weren't so beautiful, maybe I'd have more character.

REX HARRISON

There is something irresistibly comic about selfishness, egotism, and dedication to one's own well-being when it is on such a cosmic scale.

—HUGH LEONARD

ROBERT MORLEY

It is a great help for a man to be in love with himself. For an actor, it is absolutely essential. I genuinely like myself, and have no reason to believe that the feeling is not reciprocated.

★

To fall in love with oneself is the first secret of happiness. I did so at the age of four and a half. Then if you're not a good mixer you can always fall back on your own company.

PAUL NEWMAN

You know, you are privileged to have this interview.

—TO EDWIN MILLER

GEORGE SANDERS

We were both in love with him. . . . I fell out of love with him, but he didn't.

—Zsa Zsa Gabor

SYLVESTER STALLONE

I am a sensitive writer, actor, director. Talking business disgusts me. If you want to talk business, call my disgusting personal manager.

★

His diction (always bad) is now incomprehensible, and his ego has grown so big that it now fills his mouth like a cup of mashed potatoes.

—John Powers

RUDOLPH VALENTINO

I am beginning to look more and more like my miserable imitators.

SIR HERBERT BEERBOHM TREE

A charming fellow, and so clever: he models himself on me.

—OSCAR WILDE

II

PHILOSOPHERS

". . . never a greater monster or miracle . . ."

SIR A. J. (FREDDIE) AYER
British philosopher

... **W**hen someone looked up from the paper to say, "I see poor old Philip Toynbee is dead," Freddie's response was, in full, "Ah, he wrote a very nice notice of my first book."

AUGUSTE COMTE
French philosopher

What an irreparable loss!

(LAST WORDS)

JOSEPH GLANVILLE
British philosopher

Every man is naturally a Narcissus, and each passion in us no other but self-love sweetened by milder epithets.

MICHEL EYQUEM DE MONTAIGNE

I have never seen a greater monster or miracle in the world than myself.

FRIEDRICH NIETZSCHE

I'm not a man—I'm dynamite!

JULES RENARD
French writer

I find that when I do not think of myself I do not think at all.

FRANÇOIS DE LA ROCHEFOUCAULD
French writer

I am clever, and make no scruples of declaring it; why should I?

BERTRAND RUSSELL

I have a certain hesitation in starting my biography too soon for fear of something important having not yet happened. Suppose I should end my days President of Mexico; the biography would seem incomplete if it did not mention this fact.

ARTHUR SCHOPENHAUER

If we weren't all so much in ourselves, life would be so uninteresting we couldn't endure it.

MAX STIRNER
German philosopher

Nothing is more to me than myself.

III

WRITERS

"The Bible, Homer, Shakespeare . . .
and Me."

★

SHERWOOD ANDERSON

What's wrong with this egotism? If a man doesn't delight in himself and the force in him and feel that he and it are wonders, how is all life to become important to him? The interest in the lives of others, the high evaluation of these lives, what are they but the overflow of the interest he finds in himself, the values he attributes to his own being?

★

[He] purred with satisfaction at knowing that the high-brows and intellectuals of the East had taken him up. One word describing himself and his work he understood, and that was "naive." He began to use the word repeatedly in conversation and grew to be so self-consciously naive that he seemed to me to drool; he was several years getting over this attention from the intellectuals and becoming himself again.

—Burton Rascoe

★

Sherwood Anderson never tried to please anybody—he considered it everybody's duty to please him.

—Ben Hecht

★

If a girl was with us, I was sure to hear Swatty open up as a searcher for deep truths. You could tell how smitten he was with a girl by how ardently he started praising himself. He called it self-revelation.

—Ben Hecht

ISAAC ASIMOV

I am the beneficiary of a lucky break in the genetic sweep-stakes.

Isaac Asimov has written the history of the world in one volume and his autobiography in two.

—ANONYMOUS FORMER COLLEAGUE

HONORÉ DE BALZAC

It was Balzac's belief that in order to write a great book it was necessary for him to be chaste. So whenever he bedded a woman, he whispered to himself, "There goes another masterpiece."

Balzac . . . was so conceited that he raised his hat every time he spoke of himself.

—ROBERT S. BROUGHTON

AUBREY BEARDSLEY

My favorite authors: Balzac, Voltaire, and Beardsley.

ROBERT BENCHLEY

It took me fifteen years to discover I had no talent for writing, but I couldn't give it up because by that time I was too famous.

ARNOLD BENNETT

If egotism means a terrific interest in one's self, egotism is absolutely essential to efficient living.

JEFFREY BERNARD

I've always *craved* being not just a success but being well known. I don't like being just a face in a saloon bar.

JAMES BOSWELL

I think that there is a blossom about me of something more distinguished than the generality of mankind.

HAROLD BRODKEY

It is just possible I am the voice of the coming age.

WILLIAM F. BUCKLEY JR.

I realize about myself that I am, for all my passions, implacably, I think almost *unfailingly*, fair; objective, *just*.

ALBERT CAMUS

I conceived at least one great love in my life, of which I was always the object.

TRUMAN CAPOTE

I'm an alcoholic. I'm a drug addict. I'm homosexual. I'm a genius.

★

I've known all my life that I could take a bunch of words and throw them up in the air and they would come down just right. I'm a semantic Paganini.

★

Truman Capote's self-esteem was undentable.
—ANTHONY POWELL

THOMAS CARLYLE

Let me have my own way in exactly everything, and a sunnier and pleasanter creature does not exist.

RAYMOND CHANDLER

Yes, I am exactly like the characters in my books. I am very tough and have been known to break a Vienna roll with my bare hands. I am very handsome, have a powerful physique and change my shirt every Monday.

JAMES GOULD COZZENS

I'm troubled to find that people who aren't bores at all, now, if I spend any length of time with them, quite quickly tend to bore me. I have to see the horrid possibility that it won't be long now until I find no one interesting but myself. *There* I seem to find no flagging of interest.

ROALD DAHL

He was extremely conceited, saw himself as a creative artist of a high order, and therefore entitled to respect and very special treatment.

—ISAIAH BERLIN

★

The most conceited man who ever lived in our time in New York City. Vain to the point where it was a kind of natural wonder.

—BRENDAN GILL

THEODORE DREISER

Shakespeare, I come!

(INTENDED LAST WORDS)

LAWRENCE DURRELL

My problem is intense vanity and narcissism. I've always had such a good physique and such intense charm that it's difficult to be true to myself.

GUSTAVE FLAUBERT

It's splendid to be a great writer; to put men into the frying pan of your imagination and make them pop like chestnuts.

ALEX HALEY

Roots is obviously great, ranking with the Bible and Homer's *Iliad* and *Odyssey*.

FRANK HARRIS

Christ went deeper than I, but I have had a wider range of experience.

★

I am, really, a great writer; my only difficulty is in finding great readers.

★

Can there ever have been, since St. Paul, such a pompous, conceited, opinionated, patronizing ass? Patronizing Ruskin, Emerson, Carlyle, Whitman, Wilde, and the Prince of Wales; patronizing the Parthenon or the whole continent of North America; patronizing the arts, patronizing philosophy, patronizing God. Prose stodgy and repetitious; moralizing at once trite and windy; and as for the celebrated sex, orgasms going off as noisily and monotonously as a twenty-gun salute—to Frank Harris.

—SIMON RAVEN

CLIVE JAMES

I've got a *monumental* conceit, *look* at me—conceit on the rampage. I seriously believe this, you've got to keep your conceit well-brushed and ready to operate at all times.

HENRY JAMES

I know everything. One has to, to write decently.

JAMES JOYCE

I seriously believe that you will retard the course of civilization in Ireland by preventing the Irish people from having one good look at themselves in my nicely-polished looking-glass.

(TO HIS PUBLISHER)

★

We have met too late, Mr. Yeats, and you are too old to be influenced by me.

(ON YEATS'S FORTIETH BIRTHDAY)

★

[**H**e's] going mad with vanity.

—EVELYN WAUGH

D. H. LAWRENCE

I am a man, and alive . . . For this reason I am a novelist. And being a novelist, I consider myself superior to the saint, the scientist, and the poet, who are all great masters of different bits of man alive, but never get the whole hog.

FRAN LEBOWITZ

Success didn't spoil me; I've always been insufferable.

SINCLAIR LEWIS

I expect to be the most talked-of writer.

A. J. LIEBLING

I can write better than anyone who can write faster, and I can write faster than anyone who can write better.

W. SOMERSET MAUGHAM

I think I ought to have the OM [Order of Merit] . . .
They gave Hardy the OM and I think I am the greatest
living writer of English, and they ought to give it to me.

HENRY MILLER

In this life I am God, and like God, I am indifferent to my own fate.

★

Henry Miller, by his own account, is never less than superb, in life, in art, in bed. Not since the memoirs of Frank Harris has there been such a record of success in the sack.

—GORE VIDAL

ALFRED DE MUSSET
French poet

How glorious it is, but how painful it is also, to be exceptional in this world!

VLADIMIR NABOKOV

I think like a genius, I write like a distinguished author, and I speak like a child.

ANAÏS NIN

People exist for her only as pairs of eyes in which to catch her own reflection. No wonder their owners so often disappoint her. They want mirrors, too.

—GORE VIDAL

★

Her persistent fantasy is that she is Joan of Arc forever putting Dauphins on the throne. Unfortunately, whenever Dauphin becomes King, she becomes regicide—that is, when she does not try to seize the throne herself.

—GORE VIDAL

SEÁN O'FAOLÁIN
of himself and Frank O'Connor

We lived in the blissful state of amicable antagonism natural to two rising geniuses filled with sympathy for such failures as Balzac and Maupassant, who had no fore-warning of the wonder-children coming after them.

CAMILLE PAGLIA

I was a parallel phenomenon to businessman-turned-politician Ross Perot and radio personalities Rush Lim-baugh and Howard Stern, with their gigantic nationwide following. We have widely different political views, but all four of us, with our raging egomania and volatile comic personae tending toward the loopy, helped restore free speech to America.

★

I'm in love with myself. It's the romance of the century!

LUIGI PIRANDELLO

I alone am still able to write great new things.
  . . . the richness of my soul, the power of my brain, and the enormous capacity for feeling of my heart were enough for me.

(Love Letters to Marta Abba)

JOSEF PASTERNAK

I am never sure where modesty ends and supreme self-esteem begins.

—GRIGOR VINOKUR

HAROLD ROBBINS

Harold could be the best conversationalist in the world—if he ever found anyone he thought worth talking to.

—HERBERT ALEXANDER

MICKEY SPILLANE

I'm the most translated author in the world, behind Lenin, Tolstoy, Gorki and Jules Verne. And they're all dead.

GERTRUDE STEIN

Think of the Bible and Homer, think of Shakespeare and think of me.

★

I have been the creative literary mind of the century.

★

It takes a lot of time to be a genius, you have to sit around so much doing nothing, really doing nothing.

★

Yes, the Jews have produced only three original geniuses: Christ, Spinoza and myself.

LYTTON STRACHEY

Madam, I *am* the civilization for which they are fighting.
(ASKED DURING WORLD WAR I WHY HE
WAS NOT FIGHTING FOR CIVILIZATION)

JACQUELINE SUSANN

A good writer is one who produces books that people read. . . . So if I'm selling millions, I'm good.

JONATHAN SWIFT

Good God! What a genius I was when I wrote that book.
(*The Tale of a Tub*)

LEO TOLSTOY

He would like to destroy his old diaries and to appear before his children and the public only in his patriarchal robes. His vanity is immense!

—SOPHIE TOLSTOY, TOLSTOY'S WIFE

MARK TWAIN

Twenty-four years ago I was strangely handsome. The remains of it are still visible through the rifts of time. I was so handsome that human activities ceased as if spellbound when I came into view, and even inanimate things stopped to look—like locomotives and district messenger boys and so on. In San Francisco in the rainy season I was often taken for fair weather.

IVAN TURGENEV

Turgenev had the air of his own statue erected by national subscription.

—OLIVER WENDELL HOLMES SR.

GORE VIDAL

I am, at heart, a tiresome nag complacently positive that there is no human problem which could not be solved if people would simply do as I advise.

★

I've just finished reading *Henry Esmond* for the first time and much as I like the unfashionable Thackeray I couldn't help but think how much better I do that sort of book than he does.

PATRICK WHITE

My homosexuality gives me all the insights that make me a great writer.

OSCAR WILDE

I am the only person in the world I should like to know thoroughly.

★

To love oneself is the beginning of a life-long romance.

★

Nothing, except my genius.

(REPLY TO U.S. CUSTOMS OFFICIAL, ASKING WHAT HE HAD TO DECLARE)

★

The gods had given me almost everything. I had genius, a distinguished name, high social position, brilliancy, intellectual daring; I made art a philosophy and philosophy an art; I altered the minds of men, and the colors of things . . . whatever I touched I made beautiful in a new mode of beauty . . . I awoke the imagination of my century so that it created a myth and legend around me. I summed up all systems in a phrase and all existence in an epigram.

COLIN WILSON

I want to be remembered as the greatest writer of this century. I've been compared to Plato.

VIRGINIA WOOLF

Virginia Woolf's *A Writer's Diary*: usually done in "fifteen minutes before dinner." What a monster of egotism she was!

—Louise Bogan

PERCY WYNDHAM LEWIS

I am rather like Mr. Shaw might have been like if he had been an artist . . . (He said that he was a finer fellow than Shakespeare. I merely prefer myself to Mr. Shaw.)

ÉMILE ZOLA

Perfection is such a nuisance that I often regret having cured myself of using tobacco.

IV

COMPOSERS AND MUSICIANS

". . . Rubinstein, God, and Piatigorsky . . ."

★

SIR THOMAS BEECHAM

I am not the greatest conductor in this country. On the other hand I am better than any damn foreigner.

LUDWIG VAN BEETHOVEN

I, too, am a king.

LEONARD BERNSTEIN

. . . a department store of music.
—IGOR STRAVINSKY

★

He has a fatal gift of projecting himself rather than the topic at hand.
—MICHAEL STEINBERG

★

I think a lot of Bernstein—but not as much as he does.
—OSCAR LEVANT

HECTOR BERLIOZ

At least I have the modesty to admit that lack of modesty is one of my failings.

VAN CLIBURN

I'm not a success. I'm a sensation.

GEORGE GERSHWIN

Tell me, George, if you had to do it all over, would you fall in love with yourself again?

—OSCAR LEVANT

OSCAR LEVANT

I've given up reading books. I find it takes my mind off myself.

★

What the world needs is more geniuses with humility; there are so few of us left.

ARTHUR RUBINSTEIN

Sometimes when I sit down to practice and there is no one else in the room, I have to stifle an impulse to ring for the elevator man and offer him money to come in and hear me.

★

If the Almighty himself played the violin, the credits would still read "Rubinstein, God, and Piatigorsky," in that order.

—JASCHA HEIFETZ
(RUBINSTEIN ALWAYS GOT TOP BILLING WHEN HE
PLAYED TRIO WITH THE OTHER TWO ARTISTS.)

JEAN SIBELIUS

A man writing a profile of Sibelius called on the great composer and spent an agreeable afternoon noting down his views on art, life and the state of the world. Later

Sibelius took him to the station and put him on the train back to town. The man was settling into his seat when he heard a bellow from the platform. Sibelius was dashing along beside the carriage, determined to impart a final piece of information he deemed essential to the understanding of his creative wellsprings. "I forgot to say," Sibelius panted, "I have an enormous prick."

(TOLD TO ALEXANDER COCKBURN BY HIS FATHER, CLAUDE)

V

THEATER AND MOVIES

". . . ruthless and power-loving . . ."

★

JAMES AGATE
British theater critic and diarist

I don't know very much, but what I do know I know better than anybody, and I don't want to argue about it. I know what I think about an actor or an actress, and I am not interested in what anybody else thinks. My mind is not a bed to be made and remade.

★

Was Wagner charmed by Brahms? Did Balzac boost George Sand? Did Whistler crack up Sargent? Did Melba rave over Tetrazzini? Was Sarah crazy about Duse? Only the second-rate artist has time for the work of others; the first-rate artist is preoccupied with his own output, to the exclusion of any and everybody else's. I'm your first-rate artist.

FEDERICO FELLINI

Even if I set out to make a film about filet of sole, it would be about me.

SIR W. S. GILBERT

You've no idea what a poor opinion I have of myself—and how little I deserve it.

SAMUEL GOLDWYN

The directorial skill of [Rouben] Mamoulian, the radiance of Anna Sten and the genius of Goldwyn have united to make the world's greatest entertainment. This is the kind of ad I like. No exaggeration.

SACHA GUITRY
French actor and dramatist

[He] is amazed that there exists no play, no book about Louis XIV. Because he resembles Louis XIV (he says), he imagines himself to be a genius. Now, Louis XIV was a monument of stupidity. Saint-Simon and Chamfort attest to that. People placed bets at Versailles: "Is there a man in the world stupider than the king?"

—JEAN COCTEAU

SIR PETER HALL

I was described as being ruthless and power-loving by Peter Lewis in *Nova* magazine in about 1962. I have been ruthless and power-loving ever since.

HENRIK IBSEN

Ibsen challenged the reception given to *Peer Gynt* by declaring, "My book is poetry, and if it is not, then it shall be. The Norwegian conception of what is poetry shall be made to fit my book."

—JOSEF STEINBERG

DAVID MERRICK

It is not enough that I should succeed—others should fail.

LENI RIEFENSTAHL

[Her] thirst for applause, her bottomless narcissism, is worse than tedious, she is so dazzled by her own light that she notices nothing, but nothing, around her.

—IAN BURUMA

GEORGE BERNARD SHAW

I often quote myself. It adds spice to my conversation.

★

The world contrived to get on before I was born (I didn't quite know how) and I daresay it will make some sort of lame shift after I am dead.

★

With the single exception of Homer, there is no eminent writer, not even Sir Walter Scott, whom I can despise so entirely as I despise Shakespeare when I measure my mind against his. It would positively be a relief to dig him up and throw stones at him.

★

The occasion was Shaw's curtain speech after the successful premiere of *Arms and the Man* in 1894. There was a boo from the gallery to which Shaw replied: "I assure the gentleman in the gallery that he and I are of exactly the same opinion, but what can we do against the whole house who are of the contrary opinion."

★

The way Bernard Shaw believes in himself is very refreshing in these atheistic days when so many people believe in no God at all.

—ISRAEL ZANGWILL

AUGUST STRINDBERG

I was always able to preserve my great brain from the influence of my sexual instinct, so that I loved, coupled passionately, and thought lucidly all the time—and then I wrote!

OSCAR WILDE

Who am I to tamper with a masterpiece?

(WHEN ASKED TO MAKE CHANGES IN ONE OF HIS PLAYS)

VI

POPULAR ENTERTAINERS

"Everybody loves me . . ."

★

JAMES BROWN

I've outdone anyone you can name—Mozart, Beethoven, Bach, Strauss, Irving Berlin—he wrote 1,001 tunes. I wrote 5,500.

JOHN DENVER

I epitomize America.

CAROL DODA
topless dancer

I see myself as a humanitarian, whatever that means.

DEBBY HARRY

I don't mind if my skull ends up on a shelf, as long as it's got my name on it.

MICK JAGGER

I'm—along with the Queen, you know—one of the best things England's got. Me and the Queen.

ELSIE JANIS
American entertainer

I realize, at least, that I have never been really virtuous,
I have only been egotistical.

AL JOLSON

It was easy enough to make Jolson happy at home. You just had to cheer him for breakfast, applaud wildly for lunch, and give him a standing ovation for dinner.

—GEORGE BURNS

JOHN LENNON

If there is such a thing as genius, which is just what— what the fuck is it?—I am one.

★

We're more popular than Jesus Christ now. I don't know which will go first. Rock-and-roll or Christianity.

MADONNA

Listen, everybody is entitled to my opinion.

WAYNE NEWTON

Everybody loves me, everybody loves me, but the only one I want to love me is you.

LITTLE RICHARD

I have never been conceited; I'm convinced.

FRANK SINATRA

He regards his voice as an instrument without equal, and although he tries scrupulously to be polite about the possessors of other renowned voices, he is apt—if the name of a competitor comes up abruptly in conversation—to remark: "I can sing that son of a bitch off the stage any day in the week!"

—E. J. KAHN JR.

★

He considers himself the greatest vocalist in the business. Get that! No one has ever heard of him. He's never had a hit record. He looks like a wet rag. But he says he's the greatest!

—HARRY JAMES (1939)

JOHNNY WINTER

Ah just love bein' famous, and ah think anybody who says they don't is full of shit.

VII

ARTISTS

"I have astounded the whole world."

★

PAUL CÉZANNE

[He] was the embodiment of the modern concept of
the Artist as Genius, totally preoccupied with his talent
and quite indifferent to considerations of social esteem,
his own personal comfort or other people's feelings. He
was unkempt, foul-mouthed and filthy. . . . When someone asked him politely what was the subject of his submis-
sion to the Salon, he replied, "A pot of shit."

—ROGER FRY

★

It is rumored that Cézanne had trained his parrot to say
"Paul Cézanne is a great painter."

GUSTAVE COURBET

I have the entire artistic youth looking at me. At the moment I am their commander-in-chief.

★

I have astounded the whole world. . . . I triumph not only over the moderns, but over the old masters as well.

★

He calls himself "the proudest and most arrogant man in France."

—JULIAN BARNES

SALVADOR DALI

At the age of seven I wanted to be Napoléon, and my ambition has been growing ever since.

★

Every morning when I awake, I experience again a supreme pleasure—that of being Salvador Dali.

★

Bugs Bunny is the most ugly and frightening animal in the world. I will paint it with mayonnaise and make it an object of art.

★

Surrealists . . . are not quite artists, nor are we really scientists; we are caviar . . . the extravagance and intelligence of taste.

★

Terrorist of the emotions, aggrandizer of the negligible, paragon of perversity, surrealist superstar, raving megalomaniac and narcissist supreme—Salvador Dali was all these and more.

—ROGER CARDINAL

JEFF KOONS
American artist

I'm making some of the greatest art being made now. I'm taking us out of the twentieth century.

PABLO PICASSO

When I was a child my mother said to me, "If you become a soldier you'll be a general. If you become a monk you'll end up as the pope." Instead I became a painter and wound up as Picasso.

JAMES McNEILL WHISTLER

If other people are going to talk, conversation becomes impossible.

★

FRIEND: There are only two great painters; you and Velázquez.

WHISTLER: Why drag in Velázquez?

★

That he is indeed one of the very greatest masters of painting, is my opinion. And I may add that in this opinion Mr. Whistler himself entirely concurs.

—OSCAR WILDE

FRANK LLOYD WRIGHT

Architecture is the oldest and greatest of the arts. I am the world's foremost architect. Therefore I am the world's greatest artist.

★

The scene is at Taliesin, the legendary house-cum-shrine the architect designed for himself in Spring Green, Wisconsin. One of his apprentices had crawled under the Steinway piano to do some repairs on the legs when Wright walked in. Unaware that anyone else was present, Wright tidied up a few things, then walked to the piano, struck a few chords and pirouetted out of the room, singing to himself, "I am the greatest."

VIII

SPORTS FIGURES

". . . I'm always so right . . ."

★

MUHAMMAD ALI

Look at this face, ain't a mark on it. No other fighter ever looked this way. I am the greatest.

★

I am the only man in the world who can go and be loved by the Jews as much as by the Moslems.

★

I am the best. I just haven't played yet.
(WHEN ASKED IF HE PLAYED GOLF)

★

When you're as great as I am, it's hard to be humble.

JIM BOUTON

How come nobody wants to argue with me? Is it because I'm always so right?

JIMMY CONNORS

Everybody is saying that I might be the most unpopular champion in the history of Wimbledon. . . . But what do I care? Because I *am* the champion.

HOWARD COSELL

Arrogant, pompous, obnoxious, vain, cruel, persecuting, distasteful, verbose, a show-off. I have been called all of these. Of course, I am.

★

You know that no man can possibly talk like me who wasn't an educated man with a high degree of intelligence.

BOBBY FISCHER

Everybody knows I'm the best, so why bother to play?
(BEFORE MATCH WITH BORIS SPASSKY, ICELAND, 1972)

JOE NAMATH

I can't wait until tomorrow, 'cause I get better looking every day.

JOHN McENROE

My greatest strength is that I have no weaknesses.

IX

POETS

". . . perfect of myself . . ."

★

MAYA ANGELOU

I intend to become America's black female Proust.

W. H. AUDEN

TUTOR: "And what are you going to do, Mr. Auden, when you leave the university?"

AUDEN: "I am going to be a poet."

TUTOR: (since something must be said) "Well, in that case you should find it very useful to have read English.

AUDEN: (after a silence) "You don't understand, I am going to be a great poet."

GEORGE GORDON, LORD BYRON

To my extreme mortification, I grow wiser every day.

JAMES DICKEY

This will make Tolstoy's *War and Peace* look like a minor work.
(ON HIS HAVING WRITTEN TWO BOOKS AT THE SAME TIME, 1977)

ROBERT FROST

For him, as he liked to say, there was room for only one at the top of the steeple; he demanded to be the one. He was jealous of all other poets.

—DONALD HALL

★

He seems now to have taken up his residence in Washington and is all over the place, full of faking and self-satisfaction. He wanted us to know that he was a shrewd old boy—though obviously eating up the honors being paid him by the President . . .

—EDMUND WILSON

EDITH SITWELL

Were I not too kind to laugh at the cruel disappointment and envy suffered by certain poor little unsuccessful writers I would be amused by the fact that although I am now seventy-seven years of age, the unsuccessful are still thrown into what is practically an epileptic fit brought on by envy and malice at the mere mention of my name.

★

I have often wished I had time to cultivate modesty . . . But I am too busy thinking about myself.

★

Up to the time she was made a Dame of the British Empire, Edith Sitwell refused to be called anything but Doctor Sitwell, in recognition of her honorary degrees. Then the multiple honors began to pile up and create a problem which, in her own fashion, she has solved by signing herself "Dame Edith Sitwell, DBE, D.Litt., D.Litt., D.Litt."

—HELEN BEVINGTON

EDITH, OSBERT, AND SACHEVERELL SITWELL

They're aristocrats, I say, thinking criticism upstart impertinence on the part of flunkys.

—VIRGINIA WOOLF

ALGERNON CHARLES SWINBURNE

Full of mine own soul, perfect of myself,
Towards mine and me sufficient.

WALT WHITMAN

I dote on myself, there is a lot of me and all so luscious.

★

I find no sweeter fat than sticks to my own bones.

GEORGE WITHER

The seventeenth-century English poet George Wither
inscribed his satires, "G. W. wisheth Himself all happiness."

—*Dictionary of Classical Mythology*

WILLIAM WORDSWORTH

Mr Wordsworth not only exacts an entire relinquishment of all other tastes besides taste for his poetry, but if an unlucky votary chances to say "Of all your beautiful passages I most admire so and so," he knocks them down by saying "Sir, I have a thousand passages more beautiful than that. Sir, you know nothing of the matter." One's conscience may be pretty well absorbed for not admiring this man; he admires himself enough for all the world put together.

—MARY RUSSELL MITFORD

WILLIAM BUTLER YEATS

I am very foolish over my own book. I have a copy which I constantly read and find very illuminating. Swift confesses something of the same sort with his own compositions.

★

Yeats looks respectfully at Yeats reflected in the mirrors as he comes down—no, as he *descends*—the staircase of the Savile Club. I've watched him.

—GEOFFREY GRIGSON

★

. . . though at times he could be very good company, he was a pompous, vain man; to hear him read his own verses was as excruciating a torture as anyone could be exposed to.

—W. SOMERSET MAUGHAM

YEVGENY YEVTUSHENKO

. . . **a**n ego that could crack crystal at a distance of twenty feet.

—JOHN CHEEVER

★

Yevtushenko behaved like an egomaniac clown. He used Dennis Quilley and Brian Cox, who appeared with him, as his creatures. He rolled his eyes and over-inflected like the worst ham in the world. I have never seen a more dreadful display of selfishness. When they read he scratched, whispered, walked about and sipped water.

—SIR PETER HALL

X

STATESMEN AND POLITICIANS

". . . I am a glow-worm."

★

IDI AMIN DADA OF UGANDA

I consider myself the most important figure in the world.

CLEMENT ATTLEE

Few thought him ever a starter
There were many who thought themselves smarter
But he ended PM, CH and OM
An Earl and a Knight of the Garter

WINSTON CHURCHILL

We are all worms, but I do believe that I am a glow-worm.

★

History will be kind to me for I intend to write it.

★

I am ready to meet my Maker. Whether my Maker is prepared for the ordeal of meeting me is another matter.

★

Winston Churchill was never in love with anyone except himself, and possibly Clementine.

—CYRIL ASQUITH

★

[Winston Churchill] would make a drum out of the skin of his own mother in order to sound his own praises.

—DAVID LLOYD GEORGE

SIR STAFFORD CRIPPS

There but for the grace of God, goes God.

—WINSTON CHURCHILL
(ALSO SAID OF ORSON WELLES BY HERMAN J. MANKIEWICZ)

ANTHONY CROSLAND
British Labour Leader (as a houseguest)

He was always determined to put off meals until he felt sufficiently relaxed to enjoy them, and he employed his considerable armoury in delaying tactics until the meals were often an hour or so late. He closed all conversations which did not interest him, and he never refrained from complaining of any lapse in the standards of the house.

—FRANCES DONALDSON

LORD CURZON

About Lord Curzon—Lady Cynthia [his bride] could only get some of her friends asked to her wedding by inventing titles for them.

—Geoffrey Madan

★

When Curzon was Foreign Secretary, someone, wishing to telephone to his private secretary at an hour when C. had generally left for luncheon, asked, "His Imperial Pomposity gone yet?" Curzon answered the call. "Speaking," was the reply.

—Sir George Leveson-Gower

★

Curzon's political (and often personal) relations were a disaster. Obsessive, overbearing, arrogant, he failed only to put off those subordinates who continued to admire the administrative ability which lay hidden beneath the surface petulance.

—C. A. Bayley

CHARLES DE GAULLE

I respect only those who resist me, but I cannot tolerate them.

★

[Charles de Gaulle is] an artlessly sincere megalomaniac.
—H. G. WELLS

★

De Gaulle has *par excellence* the imperviable face of a self-satisfied schoolmaster: without a word, but with swollen nose and bloodhound eyes, he surveys the world around him with utter contempt.

—CECIL BEATON

EAMON DE VALERA

Whenever I wanted to know what the Irish people wanted, I had only to examine my own heart and it told me straight off what the Irish People wanted.

BENJAMIN DISRAELI

Benjamin Disraeli is a self-made man and worships his creator.

—JOHN BRIGHT (ATTRIB.)

NAPOLÉON BONAPARTE

You've got your castles to go back to if you lose a battle. I've got nothing if I'm not Emperor of the French, and I don't give a damn if I do away with a million men tomorrow as long as I stay on top.

★

My downfall raises me to infinite heights.

JOHN FOSTER DULLES

Once—many years ago—I thought I had made a wrong decision. Of course, it turned out that I had been right all along. But I was wrong to have *thought* that I was wrong.

(ASKED IF HE HAD EVER MADE A WRONG DECISION)

WILLIAM GLADSTONE

I do not object to Gladstone's having the ace of trumps up his sleeve, but only to his pretense that God had put it there.

—HENRY LABOUCHÈRE

FRANK HAGUE
former Jersey City Mayor

I am the law!

LYNDON B. JOHNSON

I am the king. I am the king.

HENRY KISSINGER

Next week there can't be any crisis. My schedule is already full.

HUEY P. LONG

I looked aroundat all the little fishes present, and said, "I'm the Kingfish."

★

My offices are pretty now . . . I have large nice rugs on all three floors . . . Only the name "Huey P. Long" adorns these offices. I am governor, mayor, king and clerk. No . . . other authority has a right to be heard.

★

Oh, hell, say that I'm *sui generis* and let it go at that.

DOUGLAS MacARTHUR

Douglas MacArthur is the kind of man who thinks that when he gets to heaven, God will step down from his great white throne and bow him into his vacated seat.

—HAROLD L. ICKES

BENITO MUSSOLINI

On my grave I want this epitaph: "Here lies one of the most intelligent animals ever to appear on the surface of the earth."

(DECEMBER, 1937)

RICHARD M. NIXON

When the President does it, that means that it is not illegal.

JUAN PERÓN

If I had not been born Perón, I would have liked to be Perón.

WILLIAM PITT, THE ELDER

I know that I can save this country and that no one else can.

THEODORE ROOSEVELT

My father always wanted to be the corpse at every funeral, the bride at every wedding and the baby at every christening.

—ALICE ROOSEVELT LONGWORTH

MARGARET THATCHER

I don't mind how much my ministers talk—as long as they do what I say.

★

. . . **t**he insistence on the undivided sovereignty of her opinion, dressed up as the nation's sovereignty, was her undoing.
—GEOFFREY HOWE

THE DUKE OF WELLINGTON

STRANGER: Mr. Robinson, I believe?
WELLINGTON: Sir, if you believe that you'll believe any-
thing.
(REPORTED ABOUT THE DUKE OF WELLINGTON)

WOODROW WILSON

How can I talk to a fellow who thinks himself the first man in two thousand years to know anything about peace on earth?

—GEORGES CLEMENCEAU

XI

ROYALS

". . . and I want dumplings."

★

CATHERINE II OF RUSSIA

I should tell you that I like to connect everything possible with myself. I thank you for allowing me to do so.

EMPRESS DOWAGER CI XI OF CHINA
d.1908

Do you know that I have often thought that I am the cleverest woman who ever lived and that others cannot be compared with me.

KING FAROUK OF EGYPT

At Cannes, a gentleman lays down four jacks. The king lays down three kings and declares four. "I am," he says, "the fourth." And he takes the pot. Another time he doesn't show his cards. "Do you doubt the king's word?"
—JEAN COCTEAU

FERDINAND I
Holy Roman Emperor

I am the Emperor, and I want dumplings.

FREDERICK THE GREAT OF PRUSSIA

My people and I have come to an agreement which satisfies us both. They are to say what they please, and I am to do what I please.

LOUIS XIV OF FRANCE

How could God do this to me after all I have done for him?

★

L'Etat, c'est moi!

SIGISMUND
Holy Roman Emperor, 1368–1437

I am the Roman Emperor, and am above grammar.

XII

ASSORTED EGOS

". . . confusing herself with God."

★

MARGOT ASQUITH

The affair between Margot Asquith and Margot Asquith will live as one of the prettiest love stories in all literature.
—DOROTHY PARKER

NANCY ASTOR

My vigor, vitality and cheek repel me. I am the kind of woman I would run from.

★

Nancy Astor—Nannie—was a devout Christian Scientist, but not a good one. She kept confusing herself with God. She didn't know when to step aside and give God a chance.
—MRS. GORDON SMITH

LORD BEAVERBROOK

If Max gets to Heaven he won't last long. He will be chucked out for trying to pull off a merger between Heaven and Hell . . . after having secured a controlling interest in key subsidiary companies in both places, of course.
—H. G. WELLS

MARISA BERENSON

I was born with a Karma and what I make of this life will put me closer to God in the next. My ultimate goal is to become a saint.

NICHOLAS MURRAY BUTLER

His conceit is consummate. . . . He has the bearing of a Roman Emperor and he honestly believes that he was born to lead, if not to rule.

—DOROTHY DUNBAR BROMLEY

SIR ALEXANDER FLEMING

I can only assume that God wanted penicillin, and that was his reason for creating Alexander Fleming.

BENJAMIN JOWETT
Master of Balliol College, Oxford, 1817–1893

First come, I, my name is Jowett.
There's no knowledge but I know it.
I am Master of this College:
And what I don't know isn't knowledge.

—H. C. BEECHING (ATTRIB.)

FRANK LONGFORD,
SEVENTH EARL OF LONGFORD

The Seventh Earl of Longford and I appeared together on British television. As the Seventh Earl was introduced to the viewers, he swung around in his chair and looked at himself in the television monitor; it was plain that he was ravished by what he saw.

—GORE VIDAL

THE REV. SUN MYUNG MOON

God sent me to America in the role of a doctor.

CAMILLE PAGLIA

Honey, I am out of your league.

(RESPONDING TO A PROFESSOR WHO ASKED WHY SHE
REFUSED TO APPEAR WITH OTHER ACADEMIC FEMINISTS)

★

You are an idiot. You are in the presence of one of the great academic feminists of your time, and you're making an ass of yourself.

(TO A STUDENT WHO QUESTIONED HER SCHOLARSHIP)

JERRY RUBIN

I'm famous. That's my job.

SIR CECIL ARTHUR SPRING-RICE
British diplomat

I am the Dean of Christ Church, Sir:
There's my wife; look well at her.
She's the Broad and I'm the High;
We are the University.

DONALD TRUMP

The reason they're giving for the divorce is that Donald Trump has been having a long-term affair with himself.
—ARSENIO HALL

TED TURNER

If I only had a little humility, I would be perfect.

(ATTRIB.)

BEATRICE WEBB

If ever I felt inclined to be timid as I was going into a room full of people, I would say to myself, "You're the cleverest member of one of the cleverest families in the cleverest class of the cleverest nation in the world, why should you be frightened?"

INDEX

Personal names appearing in plain type indicate the source of the quotation and those in capitals indicate the person who is the subject of the quotation.